# Topics

- Types of Conflict
- Collaboration Framework

CW00516449

3

# Agreements

- Engage and Participate
- Confidentiality
- Commit to make a difference

# Collaboration

By Jim Peal, Ph.D

All rights reserved. No part of this book may be reproduced or transmitted in any form or by any means, electronic or mechanical, including photocopying, recording or by any information storage and retrieval system, without written permission from the author, except for the inclusion of brief quotations in a review. Copyright 2017 by Jim Peal, Ph.D. ISBN, 978-1978327504

**Collaboration**

+Impact On Others

Insights

Behavior Shift

2

1. What is conflict?
2. When is conflict productive, non-productive?
3. What is the cost of unresolved conflict to the organization, to you?

**Brainstorm**

**Conflict**

**A difference +
a negative story that you tell yourself**

# Levels of Conflict

| | | |
|---|---|---|
| 5th | Owner | A problem to solve |
| 4th | On Board | Difference of opinion |
| 3rd | Bobble Head | Avoidance |
| 2nd | On a position | Disagreement Argument Fight |
| 1st | Out of the game | Disengaged |

# Your Attitude & Conflict

## Check Your Tude®

| | | | | | | | | | |
|---|---|---|---|---|---|---|---|---|---|
| **Sb** Sabotage | | | | | | | | | **Sv** Service |

| | | | | | | | | | |
|---|---|---|---|---|---|---|---|---|---|
| **Vt** Victim | **Re** Resigned | **Sc** Suspicious | **En** Envious | **Df** Defensive | **In** Inspired | **Cr** Creative | **Cu** Curious | **Cm** Committed | **Vi** Visionary |
| **Ad** Adversary | **Bl** Blaming | **Sr** Sarcastic | **Ag** Angry | **Fs** Frustrated | **Eg** Engaged | **Pa** Passionate | **Hu** Humorous | **Ac** Accountable | **Av** Activator |
| **Rs** Rescuer | **Su** Superior | **Cn** Controlling | **Ha** Hidden Agenda | **Ar** Arrogant | **Hm** Humble | **Tp** Transparent | **Tr** Trusting | **Sp** Supportive | **Co** Coach |
| **Cy** Cynic | **Sk** Skeptical | **Ct** Critical | **Is** Insulted | **Jg** Judgmental | **Ap** Accepting | **Cf** Confident | **Ob** Objective | **Md** Mindful | **Mn** Mentor |

Negative Intention Shadows     Choice     Positive Intention Strengths

**Conflict is difference + a negative story that you tell yourself.**

# Types of Conflict

**Personality Clashes**

**Roles & Responsibility**

**Power & Level**

10

# Types of Conflict

1. **Personality Clashes**
   - Assuming negative intention
   - Differences in values
   - Differences in style

2. **Roles & Responsibilities**
   - Priorities & Goals
   - Resources
   - Interdependence
   - Change

3. **Power differential**
   - Title/Level
   - Leadership
   - Experience
   - Education

# Personality Clashes

## Negative intention

- Assuming that the other person is trying to damage you in some way
- Intentionally creating upset or damage for the other

## Differences in values

- Each person has a different set of values about the same situation

## Differences in style

- Each person has a different way they approach and do their work – Dominance, Influence, Conscientious, Steady
- Each person has a different and non-complimentary communication style

# Roles & Responsibilities

## Priorities & Goals

- Different drivers and being held accountable for divergent goals

## Resources

- Competing needs for a limited resource pool

## Interdependence

- Cannot complete your task until someone completes their task

## Change

- Urgent change in what you are doing due to an urgency, change in role, change in how work is done, Change in metrics

14

# Power Differential

## Title/Level

- One person has a higher title or grade level in the organization

## Leadership

- The leader changes or there are multiple leaders involved with different styles and/or priorities

## Experience

- One person has more experience than the other

## Education

- One person has more education than the other

# Use the Conversation Cycle

**INVITE**
ask open ended questions

**LISTEN**
generously give your full attention

**ACKNOWLEDGE**
the essence of what was said

**INFORM**
express your views/experience

# Levels of Listening

- Distracted – Listening to self
- Focused – Listening to other
- Generous – Engaging other

# Steps to Transform Conflict

## GET INTO THE LEADERSHIP ATTITUDES

1. **Identify outcomes**

   "I'd like to talk about how we can improve how we work. Is now a good time?"

2. **Identify what happened and your story that followed**

   "This is what happened and how I reacted."

3. **Ask about their perceptions of what happened**

   "What are you aware of?"

4. **Identify misperceptions and positive intentions**

   "Now I understand your perspective."

5. **Agree on plan forward**

   "What should we do moving forward?"

# Collaboration

# Five Collaboration Styles

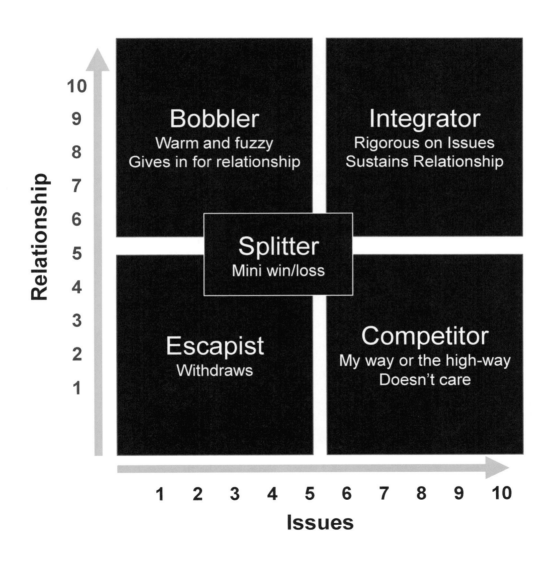

# The Bobbler

- Sees you as being on their side
- Trusting of other's intentions
- Seeks agreement
- Avoids conflict
- Seeking harmony at their own expense
- Assumes all people are looking out for each other
- Open book
- Not invested in winning
- Yields to pressure

# The Competitor

- Winning is first priority
- Fixed on own position
- Us and Them
- Makes demands
- Does not care about how you feel
- Does not trust

- Applies pressure
- Intimidates
- Judgmental
- Challenges to dominate
- Threatens, Insults, Criticizes
- Intentionally misleads
- Will use emotion to sway you

# Splitter

- Usually occurs during monetary negotiations
- Is rooted in concepts like splitting the difference
- This style places little emphasis on either issues or relationships
- It is more than likely that the real issues were never addressed
- Assumes that a win/win solution is not possible
- Involves a little bit of winning and a little bit of losing
- Is characterized by persuasion and manipulation

# Escapist

- Focuses on walking away from the negotiating table
- Withdraws and does not want to continue either the relationship or the discussion of issues
- Often blames the other party or has passive aggressive communication style
- Is usually a challenging collaboration style

# Integrator

- Starts by aligning outcomes
- Listens generously
- Sees the other's issues as mutual problems to solve
- Sees the relationship as foundational to solving problems

- Sustains the relationship while being rigorous on issues
- Works with facts & understands emotions

- Can argue the other person's point of view
- Goes to understand the root causes rather than argue points
- Drives both agendas
- Looks for options that will meet all parties' interests
- Develops multiple options
- Maintains objectivity
- Balances internal emotions
- Sees the big picture and can focus on details

# Collaboration Framework

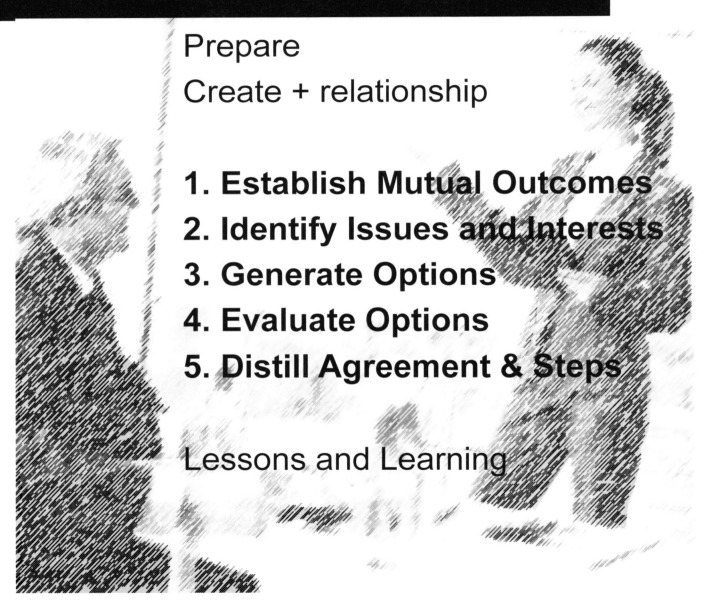

Prepare

Create + relationship

1. **Establish Mutual Outcomes**
2. **Identify Issues and Interests**
3. **Generate Options**
4. **Evaluate Options**
5. **Distill Agreement & Steps**

Lessons and Learning

Issues and Interests – for all people at the table

- Self
- Other
- Observer

BATNA

*Best Alternative to a Negotiated Agreement*

- *It is always best to work it out but if you can't then identify your alternatives to having a conversation with that person.*
- *Each alternative usually has a cost and risk.*
- *Find the one that you can live with.*

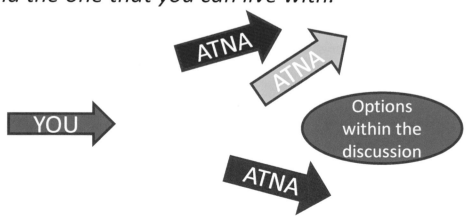

# Relationship

Relationship Tools

- Managing Perceptions
  - Take on positive attitudes
- Clean Up
  - Apology
- Rapport
  - Create a connection
  - Match and Mirror
- Effective Listening
  - Conversation Cycle
  - Generous Listening

1.  **Take full accountability** for what you did, what happened and for the perceptions, feelings, judgments and conclusions that the other person had

2.  **Apologize**. Let the other person know that you are sorry about how they were left feeling and how they were impacted (Avoid justifying or explaining your actions)

3.  **Make a promise about your future action** with regard to this event

4.  **State the kind of relationship/partnership you are committed** to having with them in the future

# Listening

- Conversation Cycle
- Hearing
- Non Verbal Encouragement
- Active Listening
- Key Words / Criteria

# Mutual Outcomes

- Identify and Agree on the mutual outcomes at the beginning of the meeting
- Agree on process
- Identify decision maker

# Real Issues and Interests

- Rather than engaging in point-counterpoint ask questions to discover the real issues and objections are in the other(s)
- Discover what is important to them - their criteria
- Let them know you understand what is important to them – drive their agenda

# Real Issues and Interests

| Issues | Interests |
|---|---|
| **What** are the issues, problems?<br><br>**How** is that a concern?<br><br>**What** are the challenges you are trying to solve? | **What** do you want?<br><br>**What** would having that do for you?<br><br>**What** is most important for you? |

*Listen and capture important criteria.*
*Replay what you heard for verification.*

# Generate Options

- Principles of brainstorming
- Think outside the box
- Creative thinking
- Momentum
- Inclusive

# Evaluate Options

- Based on criteria
- Looking at the collaboration as a whole
- Cost / Benefit to both sides
- Compare it to your BATNA

# Agreement

- Summarize agreements
- Outline roles and responsibilities
  - What
  - When
  - Where
  - Who
- Outline time-lines
- Get commitments
- Review options and consequences
- Acknowledge
- Documentation